In an age when crassness, cynicism, and outright cruelty are on the rise, Joy Roulier Sawyer reminds us that the human spirit can be refreshed in the life-giving waters of poetry. *Lifeguards* is a generous, open-hearted, affirmative book, alive to the suffering in our world but wise enough to see it all with both compassion and humor. Read it for its many pleasures, but most of all read it to feel renewed.

—John Brehm, author of
Help Is on the Way

I know of no more surer or welcoming voice into the play that is poetry than Joy Roulier Sawyer. *Lifeguards* dances across fields of the personal and the spiritual with plenty of stops for the beautiful mundane: "Give me old sugar cubes / a threadbare lime sofa." From Times Square to the Red Sea, from Saturn to Colby, Kansas, this open-heart ollection celebrates the joy of language and memory. "Becaus ᵈ this night like a / stiff tuxedo and run naked down the hal' ᵇat poetry should do…then what are we doing?

.ey, author of
Umbrell ne Eggs Cracked

Joy Roulier Sawyer's *Lifeguards* is powerfully framed by her epigraph from Thomas Merton. In this famous epiphany, Merton experienced, says his biographer, "the glorious destiny that comes from being a human and from being united with the rest...of the human race." Was Merton not at that moment a "life-guard," choosing to stand with others in solidarity and love?

Sawyer gives her readers many opportunities to make such human connections, even in the face of pain, addiction, and loss. Ultimately, though, through these poems, we experience more thankfulness than sorrow, having been deposited into "the tender hand of grace." These are resonant poems that will stay with you long after you have closed the book. Sawyer has introduced us with great humanity to many "lifeguards." In their presence we often experience healing and are never again quite the same.

—Eleanor Swanson, author of
Memory's Rooms

In the gently self-mocking "In Praise of Sentimentality," Joy Roulier Sawyer writes: "This is your own lacy valentine / candy heart pasted in the middle... / *You're one in a million. Be Mine.*" The strongest poems in *Lifeguards* actually fulfill this promise, and that is the book's irresistible charm.

The aptly named Joy is always and everywhere attentive to the lives of others, recalling small details of an aunt's appetites, or a brother's eye bruised by a baseball. In a time of deep cynicism, these poems remind us of just how important it is to imagine what really matters: the lives of other people. Stop for a few minutes, read this book, savor the lives that briefly emerge from it, and praise the writer who knows how to do this.

—David J. Rothman, author of
The Book of Catapults and *Part of the Darkness*

Lifeguards

Lifeguards

poems

Joy Roulier Sawyer

AN IMPRINT OF BOWER HOUSE

DENVER

Designed by Margaret McCullough
Photography by Amanda Tipton

Library of Congress Cataloging-in-Publication Data on File
ISBN 978-1-942280-62-0

10 9 8 7 6 5 4 3 2 1

acknowledgments

Grateful acknowledgment is made to the following journals, anthologies, and websites where these poems or earlier versions first appeared:

Bohemian Chronicle: "Your Addiction"
Books & Culture: "Growing Up with Ozzie and Harriet"
Giving Sorrow Words: "When You Leave Us"
Inklings: "On a Photo of Anne Sexton"
LIGHT Quarterly: "Two Epistolary Sonnets: *'To the Director of the MFA Program'*
    and *'P.S. To the Director of the MFA Program'*"
Mars Hill Review: "Map of the Human Heart:
    An Old Testament Chronology"
Mockingbird: "In the Year of Our Lord of the Church Split"
New York Quarterly: "Los Angeles Flashback"
Ruminate: "The Poet Answers the Journalist"
SWWIM: "Teaching Tammy Faye's Daughter to Swim"
The Beautiful Due: "Worship"
The Center for Journal Therapy: "The Poet Offers the Pharisees a
    Parabled Universe"
The Gallatin Review: "Wine to Water" and "Jeremiah Lives"
The Heart's Content: "Injury" and "St. Pauline of the Stoeckleins"
The Other Journal: "The Principled Poet Addresses the School Board"

"Wine to Water" and "Jeremiah Lives" received the Herbert Rubin Award for Outstanding Creative Writing from New York University.

"Lift Up Your Heads" was performed as part of "The Muse Project," a collaboration between the Baroque Chamber Orchestra of Colorado, Stories on Stage, and Lighthouse Writers Workshop, February 23-25, 2018.

My gratitude to bright star Chris Ransick, and to the members of the Lighthouse Writers Workshop Master Poetry class: Colette Anderson Gill, Carolyn Jennings, Joan Logsdon, Vicki Mandell-King, Jeni Rinner.

And to Scotty—husband, friend, fellow writer—your heart shines on every page, a long labor of love. I owe my deepest thanks to you, always.

III

IV

introduction

This book almost never was. About a year before its publication, the poet Edward Hirsch led a poetry workshop at my literary home, Lighthouse Writers Workshop in Denver. He handed out poems by Eastern European poets: Wislawa Szymborska, Czeslaw Milosz, Zbigniew Herbert, and others—many of whom were writing during the Holocaust.

He told us he believed American poetry had become cynical—that we'd lost, as he called it, "the poetry of affection." The poems he'd selected for us to read together made no apologies for their unabashed expressions of human tenderness, some even approaching sentimentality. "When is the last time you read an affectionate poem about a mother?" he asked.

It was then that I remembered the manuscript you now hold in book form; it had been tucked away for several years in a dark drawer of memory. After a few years of sending it out for publication, I'd become plagued with a suffocating case of self-consciousness. A few of the poems had grown to embarrass me, though they hadn't when I wrote them. But why?

All I knew was I felt uncomfortable—like a seventh-grader who enters the cafeteria and suddenly feels all eyes on her jagged, self-cut bangs and bent wire-rimmed glasses. The gold ones that clash with her silver braces. Aesthetically unfashionable.

But somehow, Hirsch's use of "affection" gently nudged me, and I remembered: *I once wrote an affectionate book.*

In Greek, the word for affection is *philia*; in the Polish, *przywiazanie*. What's notable in their translations is the emphasis on *attachment*. Although this word connotes many things, in psychological terms it's described as "a strong emotional bond that an infant forms with a caregiver, such as a mother."

Such affection implies a healthy clinging, an open-hearted need of another. And this sort of tenderness can be a subversive act in a world where the prevailing spirit is one of cynicism—a world where hardened self-sufficiency trumps human connection.

Affection speaks to us in a wholly different voice. In its tender, alluring presence, we are allowed to rest. We even become different people—more compassionate, more empathetic, more in touch with our longing for relationship, for community.

Oh yes, the soul remembers, *so this is what it feels to not stand vigilant, guarded—to not hide the heart from view.*

I had only read one or two poems in Hirsch's seminar that afternoon before I began jotting down the sources of my reticence about publishing this book. The list grew long. But its essence was this:

I feared my yearning. I feared my nakedness of soul. I feared the revelations these poems contained—poems about God, romance, infertility, addiction, my past life spent with Tammy Faye Bakker.

I'd long vowed that I would never allow false shame to impede my writing. Yet I realized I'd fallen prey to an artistic malady a friend once called, inspired by Kierkegaard, "the hipness unto death."

In Edward Hirsch's workshop, in the tender witness of two poets I particularly love—Szymborska and Milosz—I put away my shame and chose to remember and bless the poet who wrote this forgotten book.

But it was Attila Jozsef, one of the Eastern European poets we read that day, who finally convinced me to resurrect these poems. "I really love you, / believe me," he writes. "It is something I inherited / from my mother." I've included here my own affectionate poem about a mother.

It's true: I might write these poems differently today. Or maybe not. Regardless, the spirit of affection would remain exactly the same. And for that, I make no apologies to anyone—including myself.

Joy Roulier Sawyer
August, 2018

I

The Summer I Chose Water

I spent my days at the swimming pool,
until sunset slid down the sky
like orange sherbet on the cherub chins of clouds.

Lifeguard whistle silent and slack,
I learned to breathe,
learned a languid language of mellow sun and laughter.

My family hauled their MacGregor woods
to the golf course each day—grandmother, father,
mother, siblings, aunts, uncles, cousins—

diligently perfecting chip shots,
enduring water traps built long ago
on Kansas sewer lines.

Why play a game of rotten eggs, I thought—
though losing them for days on end
seemed reason enough to join them.

Still, there was the water.

Every morning,
a rush of pure pleasure
pulling me toward the tide—

I learned to listen to ocean.
He sings such splendid songs.

On a Photo of Anne Sexton

Mod print
sleeveless dress,

        elbows angling

            bracelets bangling

                cigarette dangling

pipe-cleaner leg
twined
round
and round
the other,

like a whooping crane—

as if
your laughing skeleton
will soon
flap its way
out of
that
brown
earth-bound chair

sometimes

I lay my head
on your naked,
bone-caged
heart

and listen to the marrow
run wild

The Poet Answers the Journalist

Why will poetry dance
at the break of morning?

> *Because we'll shed this long night like a*
> *stiff tuxedo and run naked down the hall*

Who knows the naked
poem's secret passion?

> *One who dresses in sheer words*
> *and removes them when necessary*

Where do undressed poems
hide when ashamed?

> *Under the shag carpet that leads*
> *to the pantry of platitudes*

What did the platitude say
when confronted by poetry?

> *I say this for your own good,*
> *and for the sake of those you love...*

How to love? How to love?
How to love?

> *Love seldom comes in the name of love,*
> *but through these strange and sweetened tongues.*

Auntie E Ate Her Way Down Broadway

and every chef in Denver knew her name.

My Aunt Eledra was first in line at Winchell's every morning,
a connoisseur of the fresh hot glazed and the chocolate cake.
That frosted blonde gobbled up the candy-sprinkled and cream-filled,
wheedled free donut holes from yawning teens pulling the early shift.

Auntie E couldn't have weighed one hundred pounds;
I stopped wearing her rick-rack trimmed shorts when I was twelve.
Her house always smelled of chocolate chip cookies,
prime rib, that creamy yellow sauce you pour over asparagus.

My aunt slapped Mary Kay masques on my face for pimples,
coached my cartwheels and splits for cheerleading tryouts,
grilled every one of my amused boyfriends
over fried chicken and homemade peach pie.

Auntie E could smack the hell out of any golf ball,
all while munching Fritos and snarfing Chik-fil-A.
"Yoo-hoo," she'd laugh as she burst through your door,
heading straight for the fridge to hunt for pastrami and pop.

Some days, we'd stroll over to China House
where the tiny wrinkled owners gave her a new nickname.
They knew "Doodah" could munch ten egg rolls plus one,
pilfered extra duck sauce to pour on a future batch.

When my aunt hit the popcorn stand for basketball games,
she'd polish off two bags and a jumbo Pepsi before halftime began.
Afterwards, she'd sweep into Chili's in her orange mohair sweater,
attack an "Awesome Blossom" like plucking a turkey for its own good.

I tell you, I was in awe of those fake diamond rings
buried knuckle-deep in grease
and Thousand Island.

But that jewelry was a ruse.

My Auntie E hurtled through Denver in a silver Lexus,
selling houses to Broncos and Nuggets,
real estate gurus and restaurant moguls,
Aurora families with screaming kids.

She'd treat you the same whether you were John Elway
or Thornton Northglenn,
sometimes played dumb with the big-wigs
and asked, "Now *what* is it you do?"

When she drove down University
she'd cross her left foot over her right thigh,
point out all the properties with a crispy drumstick
from her bucket of KFC.

She was no snob, my Auntie E.

She hustled free steaks from Outback,
plantains from Café Brazil,
savored her Brown Palace Sunday brunch
before her next-day lunch
with friends at Maggiano's.

And if Morton's molten cake was gooey-good,
she'd crack herself up doing the same damn thing, every time:
Smash the chocolate against her teeth and say,
"Ma, why don't the boys like me?"

I never got tired of laughing.

Yes, Auntie E ate her way down Broadway,
every waitress, every busboy knew her name.
Her friends in Denver ask where "Doodah" is.
They miss her.

You can understand why nothing tastes the same.

Two Epistolary Sonnets

To the Director of the MFA Program

I've never tried to write a sonnet; in fact, the mere thought
makes me nervous. I guess I'd better explain: if you knew me,
you'd know I chafe at creative restrictions. I want to be free
to put the pen to paper and say exactly what I think. (I do know a lot
of poets, though, who relish using traditional forms. When taught
the archaic Petrarchan form with its drone of *abba...cde...cde...*
it unleashed [at least for them] all that repressed, innate creativity
they already had. However, it doesn't work for me.) I've caught
a lot of flak for this, but honestly: why not let the Italians do it?
To them, it's as natural as breathing. Think of the subtle way
they've mastered the form. They're not obvious. They don't pre-rehearse
the rhyme scheme, so it's rarely contrived. Frankly, I don't care one bit
what MFA programs require. I'm just not a stuffy sonnet-writer. I'll pay
top dollar to attend your school, but I'm warning you: I only write free verse.

P.S. To the Director of the MFA Program

I hate to bother you again, but it's imperative. You see,
not only do I *not* write sonnets—I've never read Shakespeare,
either. I once saw *Romeo and Juliet*, but freaked out when she
flashed her bottom on the screen. (At 13, I was still rather fear-
ful of those things.) I knew there was no way I could hide
this fact from you people, being the poetry experts you are.
I was thinking that *even* if you offered me a full ride,
I'd have to turn it down, on principle. Frankly, I know I'm a far
cry from Edgar Guest or Ogden Nash, but I try hard. I'm slow,
but my high school basketball coach said I compensate with "scrap
and grit." (I'm an underdog, like Larry and Curly are to Moe.)
Sorry, but your "Shakespearean-sonnet-is-KING" agenda is a trap
for many aspiring poets, not just me. I hope this doesn't sound terse,
but how else do I convince you academics I only write free verse?

Stirring

When blizzards swallowed Colby,
we hunkered down and ate:
creamed eggs, chicken gravy,
potato soup and bread.

Frozen flecks of dough
spattered the windows in my room.
Snow ice cream tasted best at breakfast,
a watery paste of sugary vanilla

My brothers woke up
as Handsome Harley Race or Rufus R. Jones,
All-Star Wrestlers slamming heads
into polyester pillows,

while I pored over pictures
in TIME or LIFE—
foil-wrapped skyscrapers, lemon taxis,
Harlem fire hydrants spraying sweaty kids.

Radio KXXX crackled news
like our bowls of Sugar Crisp:
school was closed in our town.

Our town,
golden buckle on the wheat belt—

now cinched round
the thickened
waist
of winter.

Lifeguards

That summer after ninth grade,
the year I trudged each day, head down,
through the trophy-case corridor
that led to first period Algebra,

the year the high school bullies
slouched in ripped vinyl chairs,
hooted and snarled their dirty greetings
as I faded into glass—

I gave a book of my poems to Michael.

Michael the lifeguard, nineteen,
bronzed skin and hazel eyes,
signed my yearbook next to the photo
of him shooting a clutch basket.

You are a beautiful person, he said.
Please don't ever change.

I printed each poem into his own book,
red hardback, clean white pages and blue pen—
careful to write a poem just for him:

i'm sitting awake at 2 a.m., feeling bad
because someone stole your st. jude medal.
basically people are good, but sometimes clods
clog the filters of life.

I was only the basket room worker,
sliding clothes and keys and wet towels
through slots in the peeling plaster wall,

until the day Michael read his poem,
hopped over the front desk in his orange Speedo,
grabbed me, twirled me around,
kissed me lightly on the lips.

I'd never tasted gratitude before.

He placed the keys to the pool
in my sweaty palm.
"Why don't you hold these for me
until we close?" he said.
"We'll be the last ones here."

I jingled those keys all afternoon,
sang Bee Gees in my head
right up to the moment Michael
locked the doors and walked me to my car.

I'd prayed all summer the bullies
would target someone else.
But inside my Monte Carlo that day
was a pile of newspapers, rotting bananas, and eggs.

Michael grabbed the pool's metal trashcan,
polka-dotted pink with bubblegum,
stuffed it full of the stench,
hurled it into the back seat.

Then he drove straight to the culprit's house.

While I leaned against the still-running car,
he hauled the trashcan up the steps
and rang the bell.

When the boy walked out, a boy
who'd caused my knees to knock in terror,
a boy who'd shattered my thoughts into poetry,

Michael said, "I think this is yours"—
then dumped the garbage onto his front porch.

We howled all the way to Dairy Queen,
where we ordered foot-long coneys with chili
and peanut butter shakes,

sat on the still-warm roof of my car
barely touching,

as he traced my skin with his honeyed eyes.

In the Year of our Lord of the Church Split

In the Year of our Lord of the Church Split,
we stopped phoning Donna
for her recipe for sugared baked beans;
forgot Lorraine crocheted the soft blue blankets
for our newborn sons.

In the Year of our Lord of the Church Split,
we dodged one another in the poultry department,
years of picnics—glazed ham and fried chicken—
packed away carefully on ice.

In the Year of our Lord of the Church Split,
we wept alone over miscarriages, divorce;
our needles moving soundlessly through linen,
cross-stitching unbroken threads.

This was the year our husbands used fists
to hammer out the end times;
used words to sear one another
like cows.

Will Christ return? No matter.
He will find us breaking bread
in separate rooms.

In the Year of our Lord of the Church Split,
I dream of women
saving scraps of calico,

folding them into prayers.

Teaching Tammy Faye's Daughter to Swim

Cup your hands like this, I said,
and when your arm comes out of the pool,
just roll your head to the side for air

She giggled, slurped water, puffed her
chipmunk cheeks and squirted me
through gaps in her teeth

Later, we climbed out and dangled our feet,
her baby fat pooched over her swimsuit
like white-flour dumplings

Then we heard two pool workers picking up Coke cans behind us

They bought another Rolls Royce yesterday.
Makes me sick

    Wonder how many little old ladies
    paid for that

They hooted over the shrill whine of the pool's vacuum

I turned and looked Tammy Faye's daughter straight in the eye,
but she'd disappeared—

    gone scuba diving in Maui,

enough oxygen strapped to her back
so she'd never have to surface
for air.

The Principled Poet Addresses the School Board

When poets disappear,
there is no remedial course.
We read an alphabet of absence.

We are banished to concrete classrooms—
noses pressed against windows,
playground swallowed whole.

When poets fade away,
we trace a broken
braille:

our sight is felt
in the rough rub of words
subtracted.

Soon,
mute tutors of logic
grade our days;

tongues are blunt scissors,
paste,
pencil sharpener haze

for

we are deaf as adults
and dumb
is not a word we'll say—

when poets speak again.

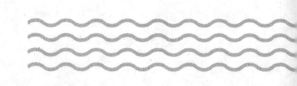

II

Jeremiah Lives

Ginsberg howled at the moon
while I was knit in the womb,
his thin, needle wail
                a clanging   cymbal
        in the night

no voice speaks for him
no voice at all.

I too saw the best minds
of the generation:

Camelot
drowned
in (*shhhhhhh*) Chappaquiddick

        a flurry, a scurry
in Laos, L.A., Memphis

four dead in O hi o.

Truth! we cried

until the tapes
told
the truth of truth

and plunged us headlong
into Saks or Gucci
or civilized Pan—

V
A sheer waste of time
the agents sniff to the guests
hushed by the beauty

The lotus and lily pad
would retreat to the garden

VI
Who will wash our hearts?
Who will weep loudly, their tears
a healing fountain?

Only a fractured moment
can fully spill a word's worth

VII
This is how poems
perfume the air, brief haikus
of alabaster shards:

Stories that are often told
begin with broken words

Interrupted Sestina, Times Square

Billy Boy, dammit. I hate the freaking way you died.
Was it that last needle in your vein—or your neck broken
when you fell down the crack-house stairs? I don't care.
So this is how it ends? This is how it ends for you, friend,
when your heart was a joyous street dance—like the bang
of those copper kettles you drummed, gleaming in the sun?

I remember you in Central Park, sitting cross-legged at sun-
set, arm around a dazed addict, promising hope hadn't died.
Later, you ate pastrami with mustard on rye, got a huge bang
out of teasing pink-haired punkers in black. Only broken
teeth hinted of your crazy past. Yet even your closest friends
missed the new signs: long sleeves in July, trips to urgent care.

We drank A & W root beer. You hugged me, said, "Take care."
You, an addict-turned-preacher feeding homeless with a sunny
volunteer like me. Bronx slum king, wheat belt queen. Friends.
We both knew grace embraces those whose dreams die
hard; knew you didn't need a heroin habit to be broken
beyond repair. Today, I heard my screen door in Nyack bang

shut, thought it was you. But it was only the awful clash and bang
between what should be, and what is. Are you free now from care,
Billy, free to fly kite-winged and laughing far above this broken
earth? Because I still flail in a fallen world, hoping each sun-
rise is my Easter, the orange-heat of resurrected dreams. You died.
So you know how I'm going to live now, Billy Boy? Friend?

Next time I see your shadowed eyes across the room, I'll roll a broken
stone away from its hidden tomb, let a choking heart breathe, let sun-
light flood the darkened place, remember your forgotten name, friend—
an absent story told in   every   empty   space.

Your Addiction

forty feather mattresses,
  piled full of snow.
    (and
    oystered
    against
    your
    spine,
    one
    grit
    of
    sand,
    refusing
    to
    pearl)

Growing Up With Ozzie and Harriet

> The trouble with normal is that it always gets worse.
> —Bruce Cockburn

It's not what they say, but what they
don't say that haunts you for years to

come; how you're afraid you will grow up
to talk too much or too little; how you are

afraid your child will cry one day and you
will say, "It's really not *that* bad."

It's not what you feel, but what you don't
feel, like a wound covered so thick with cotton

you forget it's there; how you desperately pray
to wince at the penicillin shot or the bee sting

or the arrow to the heart so you, too, can feel
alive. Sometimes in your dreams you'll look a man

in the clean whites of his eyes, tell him exactly
what you think, watch his mouth drip disbelief—

but somehow, even before you wake, you always
end up saying *I'm sorry*.

Evening Refrain

As Burt Bacharach crooned at the Paramount,
my husband and I swayed on the fourth row,
mouthed "Alfie" with grandmas in navy pantsuits.

Suddenly, I was ten again, my brother eight—
handing out iced highball glasses
to beehives and crewcuts clustered in our family room.

Scott, cowlicked, cotton haired,
impersonated Bing Crosby and Richard Nixon.
I tap danced to "Good Ship Lollipop,"
toothpick legs furiously shuffling off to Buffalo.

We'd finish the floor show with "Close to You,"
lingering on the Carpenters' haunting refrain:
Whyy...hy...hy...hy...close to you....

The blur of faces laughed, applauded.

As the room grew slurrier, we'd race upstairs,
plop on my four-poster and practice our Burt.
First, "Raindrops Keep Falling on My Head,"
followed by "I Say a Little Prayer for You."

One night, when the voices downstairs forgot to go home,
Bacharach inspired our very own top 40 hit,
surely destined to climb the charts alongside his:

Every morning when I wake up
I see Lolita sitting up
And she asks me, "Dear, how do you feel?"
I say, "Never feel fine."

For years,
My brother and I sang that refrain,
crescendoed, glissandoed, harmonized
long into the listening night:

Never, never, never, never, never
nah nah nah nah...

Never feel fine.
Oh, never feel fine.

Do we not disguise our faces and souls
and on our knees
pretend we're someone else?

I don't know about you, Supplanter,
but the limp I have
reminds me
there's someone stronger than I.

I don't know about you, Joseph,
but those divine dreams
often twist through labyrinths
of pain, fear, shame, smears, tears,

cellmates who forget
you once unlocked the chains
around their souls,

jealous brothers who despise
the fuschia/orange/cobalt way
you wear your love for father.

But like you, I've got to move on—

out of the bondage,
out of Egypt's heart-demands,
out of the smothering arms
of my Pharoahed self.

Sweet Moses. Thank you
for the love-pang of the plagues.

Real love is bloody, smelly.

Real love is a Red Sea
that takes a miracle to cross.

But tell me: did your heart stutter too?

Did your soul ever trip
over intentions and deeds
like your tongue
tripped over words?

Why do we buck
every time
you lay the law down?

Joshua, I need a final trumpet call
around the walls of my heart—

a brassy blast
to flatten that fortress
I've built, brick by brick,
for so many years.

I know you can't help but judge this:
Every 400 years I wander.

Every 400 *seconds* I wander.

Everything looks right
through my own eyes.

I no longer weep
when I see Moloch
swallowing the powdered baby
of our innocence,

I no longer choke
when I smell the stinking sulfur
of our bodies
lust-sacrificed to Baal.

I live for those glimpses
through the dark glass:

weeping like Hannah,
listening like Samuel,

but then that Saul-heart
rears back
and throws a spear,

or that David-heart
sneaks back
and takes a second look,

or that Solomon-heart
splits itself
equally in two.

Oh God, make my heart a prophet.

Let it mourn, let it lie on its side
and throw cow dung if it must,

but shout my grief so loudly
I'm either scattered
or made whole.

We are yours
for such a time as this.

We are your temple,
but rebuild these
crumbling walls.

Let all these ancient wanderings
Let all these strange silences

Let the voice crying out
in our wilderness

lead us

home.

Injury

Hazy June, smudged sunset,
Young Memorial Baseball Field, bottom of the fifth.

I wasn't in the rickety aluminum stands
when Billy Barker hurled the wild pitch,
hit my brother square in the eye. But somehow I knew.

I knew the split second our ivory '69 Caddy
lurched too quickly into our driveway,
shuddering black exhaust, that my brother was hurt.

I remember this much: my father staggering up the walk,
a gangly burden in his arms. An oval grass stain
on the right knee, one striped sock
pushed down to the shoe. A dirty shoelace undone.

All week it was touch and go,
eye swaddled thick in greasy ointment
and gauze; bedroom dark as pitch. And such awful quiet.

Not until old Doc Marshall
finally unwound the bandages,
my brother blinking, smiling, nodding his head—

did we know he would heal, play baseball again.

This past October, World Series,
Phillies vs. Rays.
Top of the ninth.

When Chase Utley smacks the ball hard
down the second base line, past the shortstop,
past the fresh young fielders diving into grass,

I suddenly remember—
not the bruised twilight, the car door slamming,
the low, hushed tones of my mother's voice,

but the *feeling*,

the one that returns to me
in odd moments, both sweet and hard:

how I would gladly
pluck out my own eyes
if it meant my brother could see.

Worship

One summer,
when the sun turned a bronze enemy
and wheat stalks shriveled
like shrunken heads,
Donald bequeathed us a garden.

Donald, elfin, nerd science glasses,
adopted us when I was twelve;
faithfully showed up each night
for my mother's lasagna and hamburger pie.

All day, he watered Colby's clay planters
of fuschia and white petunias,
but evening Sabbaths were squandered
on our backyard,
designing his own hallelujah:

a crystal waterfall, iced daisies,
a tangle of juicy strawberries ready to take and eat.

I'd sample and swoon and praise and applaud.
I'd exclaim and whoop and holler and sigh.

Donald beamed like a high-powered alien,
hovering, zipping, bouncing from side to side,
a human pogo stick at play.

In mid-July,
purple Easter eggplants dotted our lawn
for no good reason,

no good reason at all

so

I will never bow to the sun god
or accept his rule of scorching sorrow.

The Poet, Poor in Spirit and Such,
Banks on the Lost Coin

Say you were a lost coin.
A French guinea, perhaps.

A purpose-driven life walked by,
but was hunting for purpose,
not coins.

The peace and justice folks examined you,
but mistook you for a temple trinket
from the televangelists.

The charismatics prayed to reverse
your "lost coin family curse."
No change.

Michael Moore's dolly rolled nearby.
Steve Bannon wasn't even in the neighborhood.

Someone stood right over you
and read *The DaVinci Code* aloud.
Women walked away, empowered.

You felt strangely unfound.

But then Monet and O'Keefe and Rembrandt
whispered across the room,
followed by *The Idiot* and *Jane Eyre*.

David Wilcox, Peter Himmelman, Neil Finn—
hundreds, singing us all straight to you.
Foolish men.

And if it's
Mary Oliver and friends who scoop you up,
deposit you into the tender hand of grace—

Well.

You *could* find yourself
an accomplice
in a caper quite odd.

Lost coins
can't be coin
collectors,

can they?

III

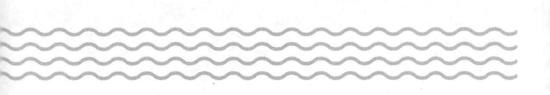

III

Los Angeles Flashback

Summer, 2016

I
I was in LA the week before
and felt the tremor of the Big One,
electric jolts up the leg and sea-sickness.
I kept alert for the fissure,
the parting of the rocks and the sea.

We all want to be swallowed by red earth,
maybe teeter on the edge.

II
Did you count how many times
Rodney rolled over
and
over?

It is time to sleep,
but I roll over
and over.

Night sticks.

III
Flames splatter blood
against a bone-white
moon. The thick rope
of smoke chokes
the city.

IV

My cousin called this morning to say
she dressed her husband
in glossy black riot gear,
his first big assignment as a new cop.

Just like suiting up
she says
Just like suiting up
for the varsity!

V

Bombs bursting
dawn's early light
my Uncle Sam shuffles
to the left
                    to the right

VI

The Italian grocer
knelt on the glass-sharded asphalt,
holding his sides
to keep his bowels from spilling out.

He froze there, mute,
unable to tell the looters
why the rows of green olives meant so much.

VII
Don't cry,
said the Man to the Woman,
belly quaking and rolling,
head heaving off the bed.

Try to buck up and be good—
even when your own flesh is ripping,
even when justice is born blue and buried,
like a thousand times before.

VIII
Here we all are:

yellow pencils tucked behind the ears,
poking through the rubble,
looking for the fault line.

The Problem of Color

What I thought about in the meantime,
between the one silver hair
and the slow syrup
of Revlon's Chokecherry stain,

is how we cover and conceal,
deftly finger errant strands,
flee the mirror until we forget.

Why I direct my gaze at you is another matter,
it seems. The angled bob, the glossy, lacquer black—
who cares what's real or not? I need relief.

You wear red sequins. I don't know the designer's name.
Color disappears where the rainbow begins.

Dearest Book Lover

What if we were to reimagine our static story, discard the prose-flattened plot of how your pleasingly predictable character is experienced by the reader? Let's begin with a fatal flaw, foreshadowed on page 73 of your clean, nicely-structured manuscript.

Can't you see the possibilities, I'd whisper in your ear on the beige sofa, *all that glorious beauty waiting to be discovered in the hidden bruise?* I'd quietly tiptoe off to the kitchen to pour you a glass of crisp Chardonnay, while your character pondered his next, unexpected move.

What if, you'd think, *what if the protagonist weren't bound by the constraints of sweaty phobias, the fear of life's unpredictable stray coral lipstick on the shirt collar? What if he saw himself a Kerouac, rocketing the unfamiliar highway like a jubilant jock of all trades, his hand steady-sweaty on the wheel as he hurtled far, far from home?*

Yes, I'd say, returning with two chilled glasses of wine, handing one to you. *That's precisely what I was thinking this story needs.*

You'd continue to muse, this time aloud. *And what if how that stammering seventeen-year-old felt when the sunny blonde turned her head away from his kiss wasn't the end, but the beginning? What if he didn't stop there, refused to surrender, wrote her letters, then poems, then finally entire books across the miles and years that left her moonswooned, heart-knees trembling?*

Imagine that, I'd say. *And what if those small, insignificant wounds weren't allowed to fester underneath his skin as if they defined him, sinew and soul? What if he didn't wear a large, loud sign across his forehead that read, "Our Sacred Man of Perpetual Rejection"?*

But he doesn't wear a sign, you'd say.

Exactly, I'd respond, sipping my icy Chardonnay, *and I simply don't read this character the way you read him.*

I think he's a wild lover afraid of his strength, afraid to ardently pursue the love interest because his too-muchness will strip the memory of his passionless father (or mother, or girlfriend, or fill-in-the-blank) naked and ashamed.

Tell me more, you'd say, rolling up your cuffs.

I mean, why not let us in on his deepest secret, that he is unrelenting, unstoppable, the last knight astride the dark horse, the last bloodied, bow-legged fighter reeling in the boxing ring? Because, after all, longing for true love is war.

Yes it is, you say, swirling the wine in your glass. *Real love is a job for real men. With traceable scars.*

Yes, dear reader, I say, setting my chilled goblet on the glass coffee table. *Dearest book lover, it really is.*

So what if I were to really *read your starched-shirt novel,* I murmur, leaning toward you.

Slowly, ever so slowly unbutton that buttoned-up story of yours, read you and read you and never stop reading you, you and that sweet, pure begging in your eyes?

The Drive

These are the things I will miss I
said, the way a tiny sock fits on

the foot like a thimble; a needle would
never pierce it, I said. I would see to

that. Names—your grandmother's,
my aunt's—Irish wrapped like an

olive blanket around the joined
flags of our flesh; the glimpse

of your brother, long gone, caught
like a butterfly in an ear, or an

eyelash. These are the things I
will miss I said, eyes dancing a

polka at the sight of a newborn
collie, fingers laced like a basket to

cradle damp-chick fur; someone
else eating Raisin Bran before

bed, knowing some genetic building
block happily smoothed itself into

place and what its bowl now holds is
you; how sleep curls around a baby like

a cat; whiskers of dreams, little
mews in the dark, the voice growing,

singing, telephone wires of time, stretching
across open spaces, our little stanza

left when we're gone. All this I
will miss I said, gazing out the

window at sharp curves of Colorado,
cradling the moon.

And this is what I will miss
you said, the joyful white

noise of drums pounding from
the basement, interrupting the

complacent slumber of our
interrupted home.

Heavenly Bodies

Saturn hung sideways
unstraightened halo

airplane slicing
silver gashes

silk champagne rain
soaking skin

stars spilling
on a bed spread

with

the plain cotton
tangle of you

Lucifer's Email

> It was by gravity Satan fell.
> —G.K. Chesterton

I re-invented myself twice, you see—
once, when I realized Jesus cared
about nothing I did:
say, Florida's hanging chads,
or exclusive rights to managed care.

Yes, I knew plenty about what he *didn't* want;
it was his desires that remained a mystery to me.

So when I confronted him, all deadly earnest
and (I thought) foreboding,
asking him my rhetorical question,
I wanted a serious answer.   And I got one.

When he split the desert air
and my burning ears with laughter,
desperately trying to answer me, but,
being doubled over, simply unable to do so,

I learned my lesson and, quite frankly,
nothing could have disturbed me more.
I realized *exactly* what he wanted.

So this time I've determined HE WILL NOT PLAY!

Since he is no longer physically roaming our earth,
scattering his wanton seeds of insidious joy,
I believe we can work together
to stop this blatant corruption of virtue.

Yes, you too can take part in the marriage of dark and light,
a moral majority for the Donald and Hillary alike,
if you will but email this warning to one hundred friends.

Friends like the ones who published this poem.

—Lucifer@hell.com

The Poet Offers the Pharisees
a Parabled Universe

Poetry

is the leper
leapfrogging!
to give thanks

the prodigal
leg-wrestling
Big Brother

the last word
you'd invite to
tea.

Poetry

is the mustard seed
that quakes
the earth—

so help
our
unbelief.

Holiday Benedictio

This
blessing,
may the advent
of family be
sheer holly.
Or is anyone among you
alone? Let him hope, for
faith is singing evergreens.
May twinkle untangle your darkness.
May your children gleefully rip open
the gift of glory. Go tell it on all
your looming mountains:
joyful, joyful pears of love
are ours
this part-
ridged
season.

In Praise of Sentimentality

Give me old sugar cubes
a threadbare lime sofa
a heart bleeding needlepoint
or *McCall's* paper dolls.

Give me Tony Bennett and a dry martini
your faded Little League photo
your campaign poster for Student Council:
Vote for me and I'll set you free.

So you're proud to be an American
sing "Stardust" in the shower
cry at the end of *Casablanca*.

Let's be honest: there are days
when everything *does* taste better
with Blue Bonnet on it.

This is your own lacy valentine
candy heart pasted in the middle
Crayola message scrawled inside:

You're one in a million. Be Mine.

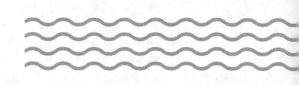

IV

VI

Fathers

There are so many. Trying so hard.

There was the one who,
puffing pure oxygen
and popping anti-nausea meds,
suddenly took up knitting.

He sent the nurse to purchase
skeins of sage and saffron wool,
knit a shawl for his only daughter.

There was the gay professor,
who, when his shy student
finally danced into his arms
with her diploma,

broke down sobbing—
so grateful poetry blessed him
with progeny.

There was the young skateboarder
I jogged past in Central Park.
He knelt over his broken-armed buddy
and said, "I'm here. And I'm not leaving."

There is my own father, restless with a remote,
flipping through Rockies and Red Sox
before he looks at me and says,
"I've made a lot of mistakes."

There is last Father's Day,
as I watched my husband
feed his father ice chips,

say, "You can go now, Dad."
We'll be alright. I promise."

All the fathers, everywhere, always—
trying so hard
to leave us all something
behind.

Shalom Moment

Because it was my sophomore year, your senior,
      two weeks before homecoming dance,
and our next-door neighbor
      sewed my red-and-white checked dress;
Because we spent Saturday in Lindsborg, Kansas,
      eating Swedish pastries, sipping coffee,
and watched your friend Lea Firestone
      throw his first college touchdown;
Because I-70 at midnight
      stretched like a black river before us,
while Stan and Susan slept in the back seat,
      letter jacket bunched in a pillow;
Because America sang "Daisy Jane" on the radio
      Does she really love me, I think she does...
as your arm crept slowly
      around my shoulder, my shining hair;
Because your scent lingers every September,
      sure as cottonwoods melt into cinnamon;
Because the heart knows
      how rare is the open mouth of heaven.

St. Pauline of the Stoeckleins

St. Pauline of the Stoeckleins
worked graveyards at St. Thomas Hospital,
dispensing 7-Up, lime Jello cubes
and love.

Pauline prayed for us daily at Mass
as Jesus glared from the stairway,
chest ripped open to display
a bleeding heart lashed with thorns.

It is said she prayed so hard
the statue eventually dissolved into laughter,
the Christ of bedpans, the one who sneaked us
homemade fudge brownies at midnight.

Pauline soothed fevers until seven,
came home to fry up egg sandwiches
for MikeMarkDavidDale
LindaMaryPaulTed.

Afternoons, she mended, patched, hemmed.
Her eight kids wore the coolest blue jeans
at Sacred Heart Catholic School.

At Christmas, Pauline taught her family
to grab forks, spoons, anything—
wrap them up, place them under the tree.

In high school, I kissed her son Mike,
joked with Mark, danced with Dale.

But it was Dave I almost married.

When we left home for college,
she sent packages filled with
Toll House cookies and Breck shampoo.

Even when Dave and I parted ways,
Pauline sent the Prayer of St. Francis
on a laminated card,
sealed the envelope with a kiss.

I didn't know she was dying.

One Mother's Day, I came home
to hold her hand as she sipped water
through a paper straw.

And though she knew
I'd never wear her netted bridal veil,
never take her name as mine,

Pauline's eyes were blue votives—

eternally bright with prayers
for me, and for her son.

Wine to Water

> For this reason I say to you, her sins,
> which are many, have been forgiven,
> for she loves much; but he who is
> forgiven little, loves little.
> —Luke 7:47

We are emptying the bottles today,
my mother and I,
pouring that amber death down the drain
with unrestrained
hilarity!

Did other children know
enemies as fierce
as those glistening glass traps
of poison were to me?

Bottles filled with hidden words,
words I'd never heard
until she'd
drunk them

and they'd mushroomed inside
like some giant fungus,
foul and deadly,

finally spewing from her mouth:
thick, heavy, blue-violet,
scribbling the air with purple pain.

I often peered forlornly
at that liquid held to light,
and wondered if I might
strain out
those awful words

and leave just the stinky stuff
for her to drink.

Yes, just the words. Not her
rollicking laughter,
awakened by gin and ice cubes,

my Judy-mom who played the piano
downstairs at daybreak
for slurry-worded lawyers and doctors,

while I, Liza-legged,
sang along quietly in my bedroom
as she played and wept,

played
and wept

at her rainbow's end.

I think that's why
they don't understand,
that upper-crust toast of the town
who no longer come to dinner

because my mother now invites
the lame and the blind
and the naked.

They don't understand why
the desperate come in droves
to drink in hope,

gulping down pitchers
of living water
she now pours
with gracious ease.

Oh, how the Pharisees denounce her!
Grimly warn Sunday Schools of her danger!
Remind their children *stay away*...

But Mary Magdalene
is *my* mother,
and I believe her,

for she weeps new tears
when she tells me
clear-eyed and sober,

she has no law but love:

for love has bought her,
won and wooed her, filled her—

and she is the forever debtor,
spilling herself out for the one
who emptied his all for her.

New wine, she tells me,
not fit for old wineskins.

Yes, I wish I could tell them,
those who refuse miracles,
as I watch the blue words
and amber death
disappear forever down that drain.

For liquid Love gathers me
in her arms and squeezes tight,
so tight I bite my lip
to contain orange laughter,

and in my heart
I rehearse
for the millionth time
my lines
for the high school firing squad:

All I know is
she who once stumbled
through my life, blind—

now sees

me.

Ocean, Cradled

Surf-swirl
after surging storm,
tendrils of fronds
fasten, loosen,
suckle shore.

Morning melts
to midnight,
nightlights nipple
a satin ceiling.

Milk-foam froth
of rocking waves—

laplaplapping
lap of the ocean,

laplaplapping lapping—

cool, cool hand
of the ocean
on your brow,

and the calm.

Resurrection Ache

What they don't tell you
is the very instant
you awake,

startled, from your slumber,
turn your head

toward flickering light;

the second you stretch
toward daybreak's
bright annunciation,

you will catch sight of a shadow.

See her there? On the wall,
a shuffling convict in chains.

What you do next is entirely up to you.

You could hum, meditate, levitate,
repeat the mantra
that darkness is only an illusion.

Call the psychic hotline, ask for George,
learn why Uncle Clem's shadow
still shakes the family tree.

Pray, picket, lobby, sing.
Forget you ever glimpsed
anything but your shining self.

See, what they don't tell you about
resurrection

is how it heals:

how hardened stone splits wide
as you stride
straight into Easter's ache

to call the shadow by name.

Your name.

How darkness dissolves
in the heat of your pitiless gaze.

Lift Up Your Heads

—in response to the Muse Urania

Here, your galaxies and Galileo,
Cassiopeia, constellations, cosmic dust,

your particle physics and Pegasus,
anti-matter, Andromeda, asteroids,

and the slow sigh of Saturn

and Hawking's heavenly body.

Lift up your heads.

See what spins and flares
on the twirled skirt of the universe:

gravity's dance, a romance,
your head resting
on the black jacket of evening.

And here, above you, look—

silver ceilings
and Jupiter's moons,

bright balloons
swooning

over the kiss
of science and faith,

unhindered by blinded parents.

Muse of imagination, your writers
one tiny grain of sandshine
come to earth—

heads in the heavens
swim with stardust,

words float free
on tranquility's sea.

Come see
what bard's handcut stars
make heaven's face so fine,

what poet wraps herself
in the blueblack carbon paper
of improper night:

comets unfastening her hairpins,
angel hair shaken loose.

The words of your writers—see them?

Driving mad across the Milky Way,
fabulous yellow roman candles
streaming interstellar dust,

or still earthbound on the hard ground
of the road, wildness within, waiting
for your great diamond of Orion.

Lift up your heads.

Muse of the spirit, your flame
one tiny thunderspark
come to earth—

tongues of fire alight
on hopeful heads,

dreams burn bluebright
in sapphire night.

Our dreams climb the heavens.

Our dreams climb the red clay of Mars,
every cratered heart exalted;
every raised and ruddy fist laid low.

Daughter of memory, do you remember?

You once lay on your back
in City Park at midnight,
face upturned,

saw Perseid spray silver showers
of champagne.

You once spread a linen tablecloth
on Golden's gilt grasses at noon,

stretched out your fingers
and said *yes*

to the thin platinum ring of sun,
set with a black pearl orb.

Today, a meteor hurtles
toward Clio's hard kiss.

The super blue blood moon
marries the blueblack night.

Lift up your heads. We lift them up.

Stardust croons in your ear.

Here they are, see the heavens now, love—
everything, always, forever,
waiting for you.

Waiting for you: diamonds.

Your diamonds.

Waiting.

When You Leave Us

When you move wordlessly
from one life into another,
you bring all who ever declared our love—
with our hearts, with our mouths.

We each see a new maple, a bush on fire,
a tiny sparrow perched on a flat rock.

Though you've made your entrance into a new home,
our old homes are filled with things you loved.
You live on mantles, in journals, on recipe cards
smudged with sugar cookie dough.

Is nothing nearer than love itself—
even when this life carefully tucks you in,
closes your bedroom window,
whispers its soft goodnight?

When midnight falls,
we are certain you hear our voices,
low and full on brick patios,
ice cubes swirling in our paper cups.

If we listen carefully,
underneath the crickets
and the murmur of twilight,
we will hear you breathing—

as steady
as this slow dance that begins among us,
underneath patient stars.

Joy Roulier Sawyer is the author of a poetry collection, *Tongues of Men and Angels*, as well as several nonfiction books. Her poetry, essays, and fiction appear in *Books & Culture, Gallatin Review, LIGHT Quarterly, Lilliput Review, New York Quarterly, St. Petersburg Review, Theology Today,* and many others. She holds an MA from New York University, where she received the Herbert Rubin Award for Outstanding Creative Writing, and teaches at Lighthouse Writers Workshop in Denver.